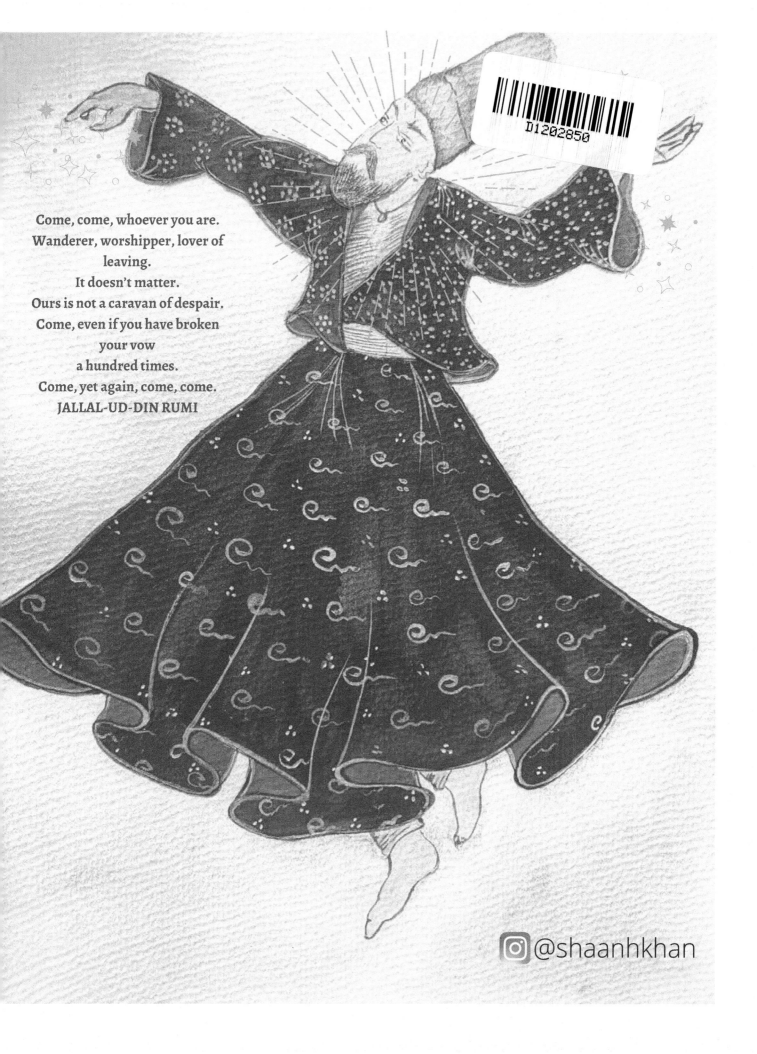

Come, come, whoever you are.
Wanderer, worshipper, lover of
leaving.
It doesn't matter.
Ours is not a caravan of despair.
Come, even if you have broken
your vow
a hundred times.
Come, yet again, come, come.
JALLAL-UD-DIN RUMI

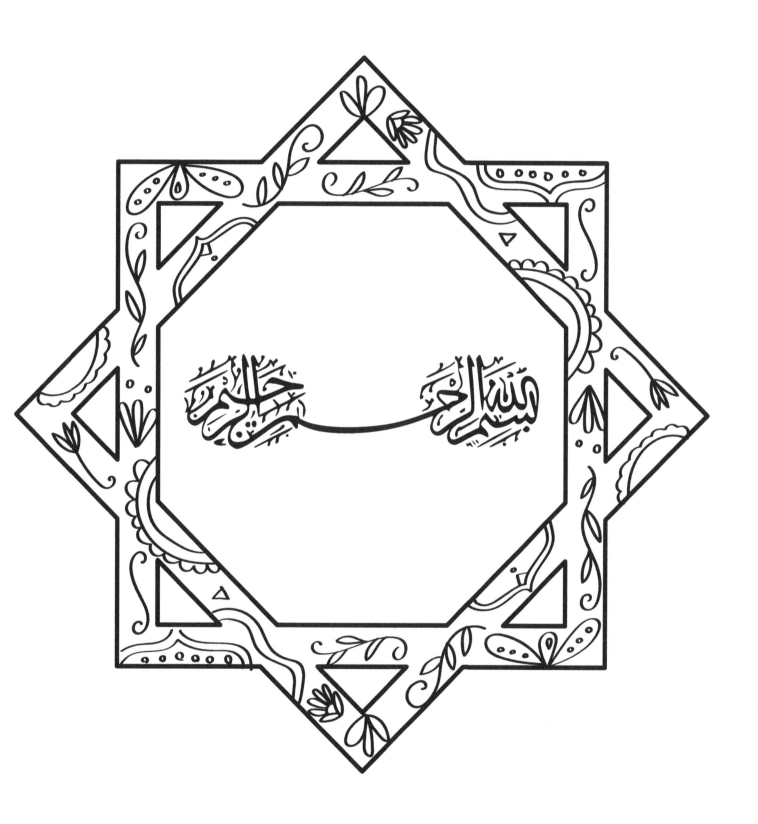

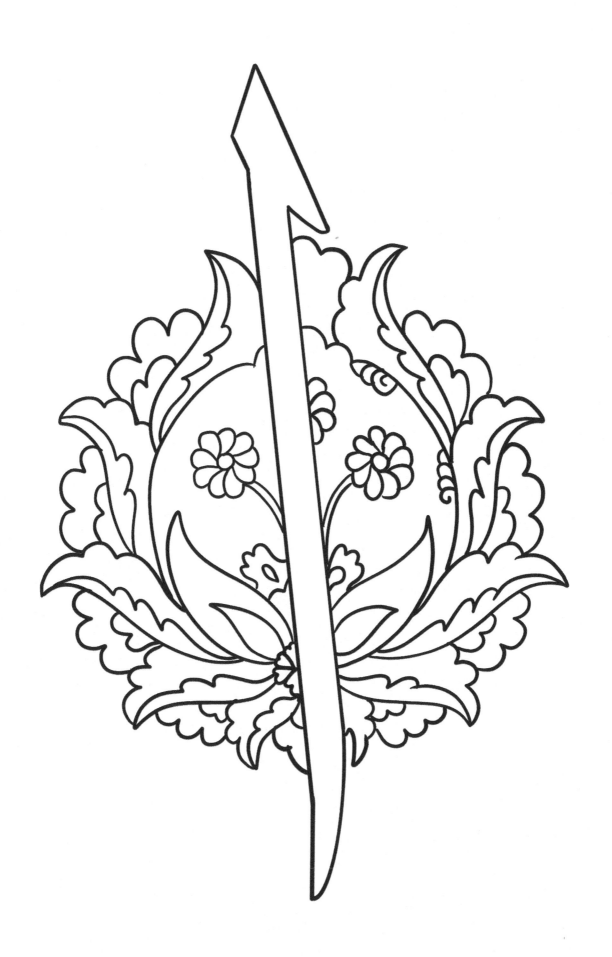

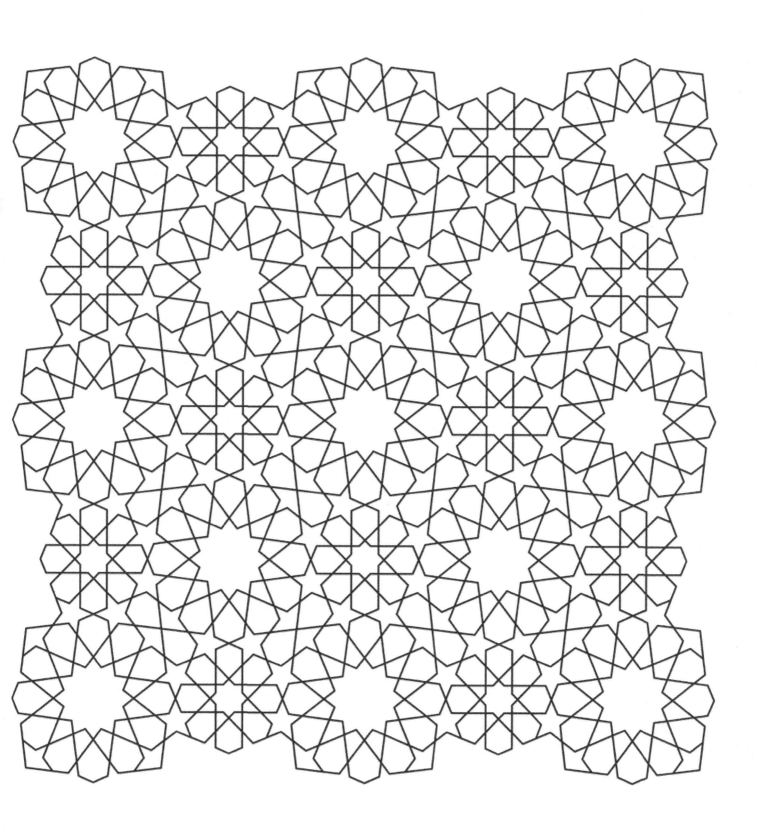

FORGIVING MYSELF AND OTHERS FREES MY HEART

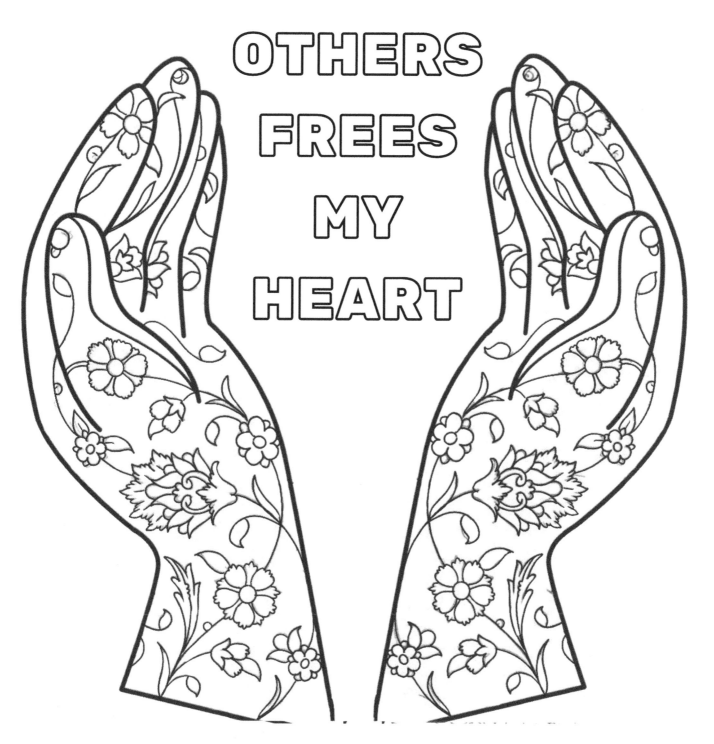

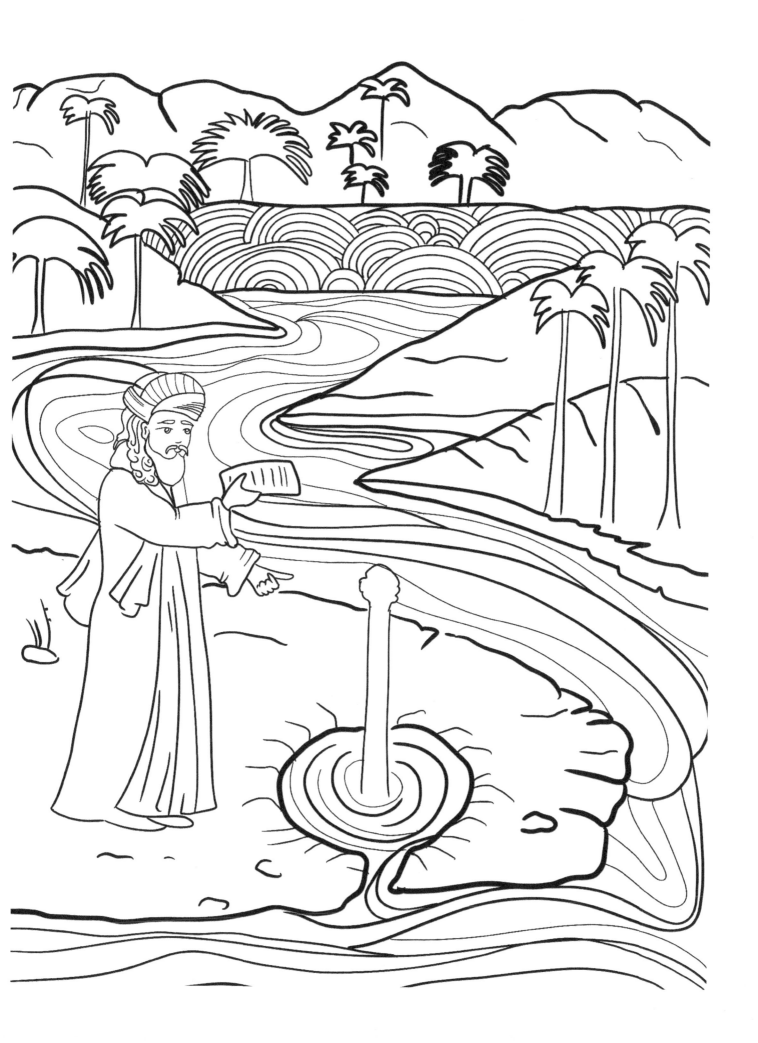

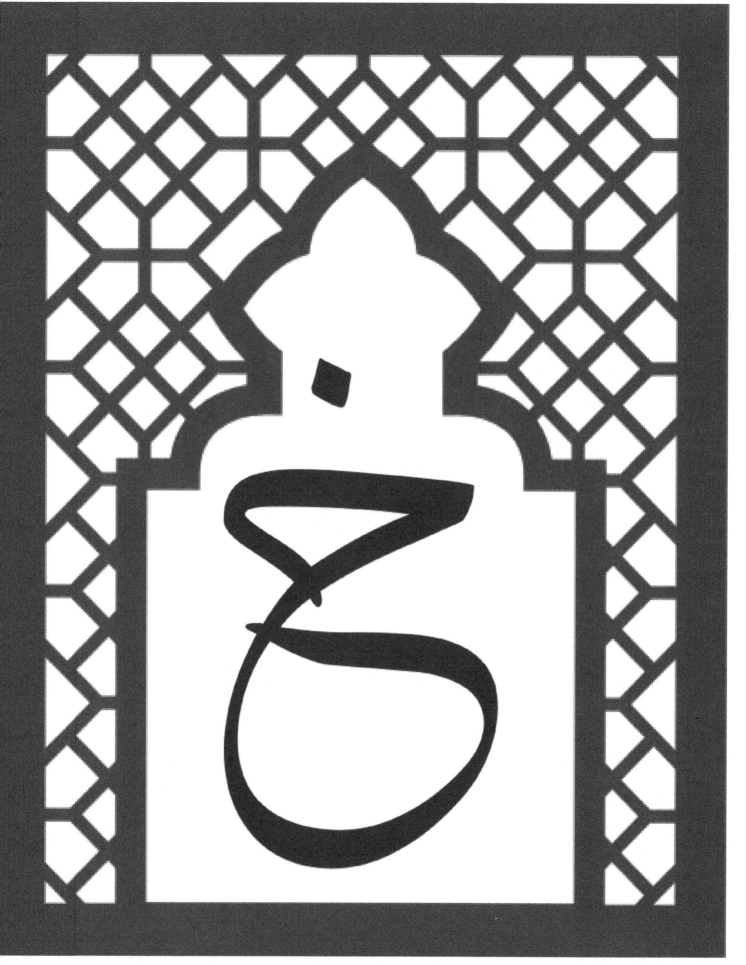

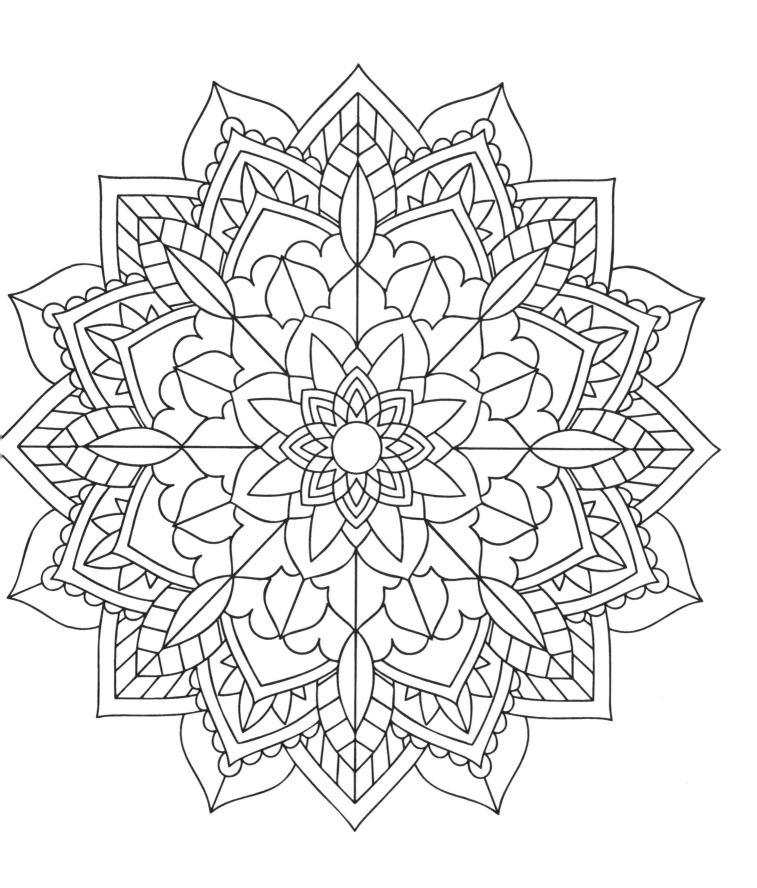

MY
HEART IS
OPEN TO RECEIVING
MIRACLES

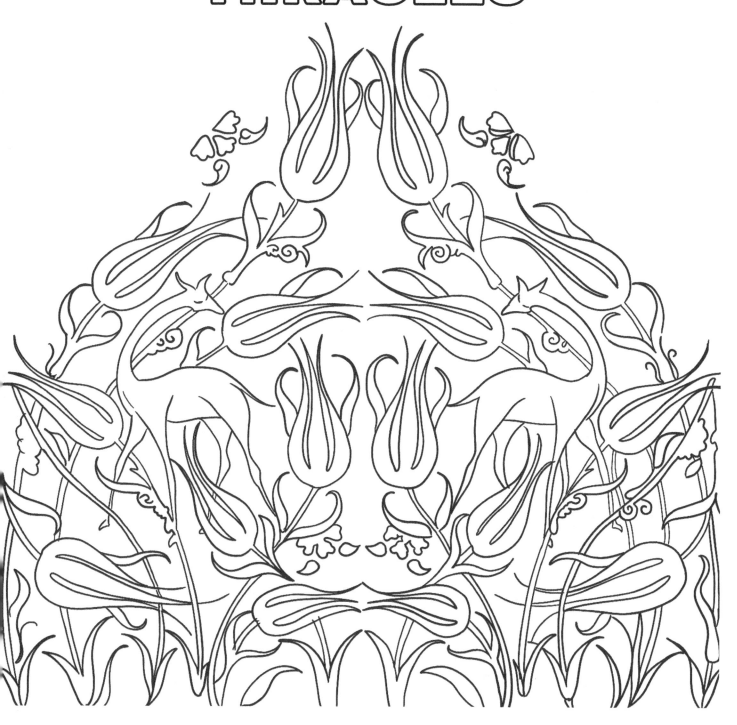

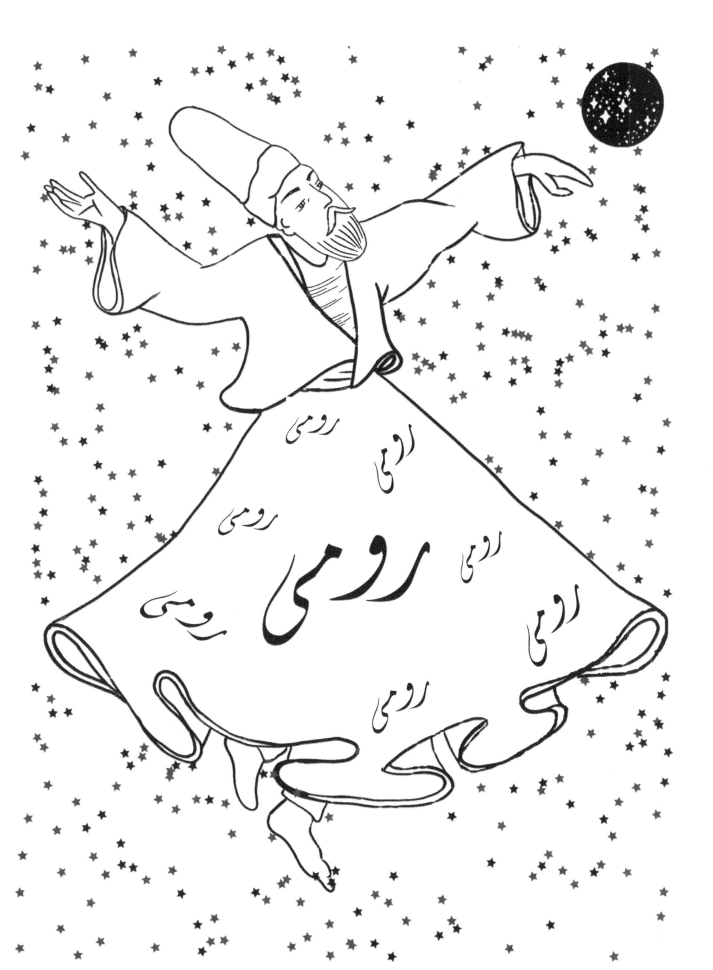

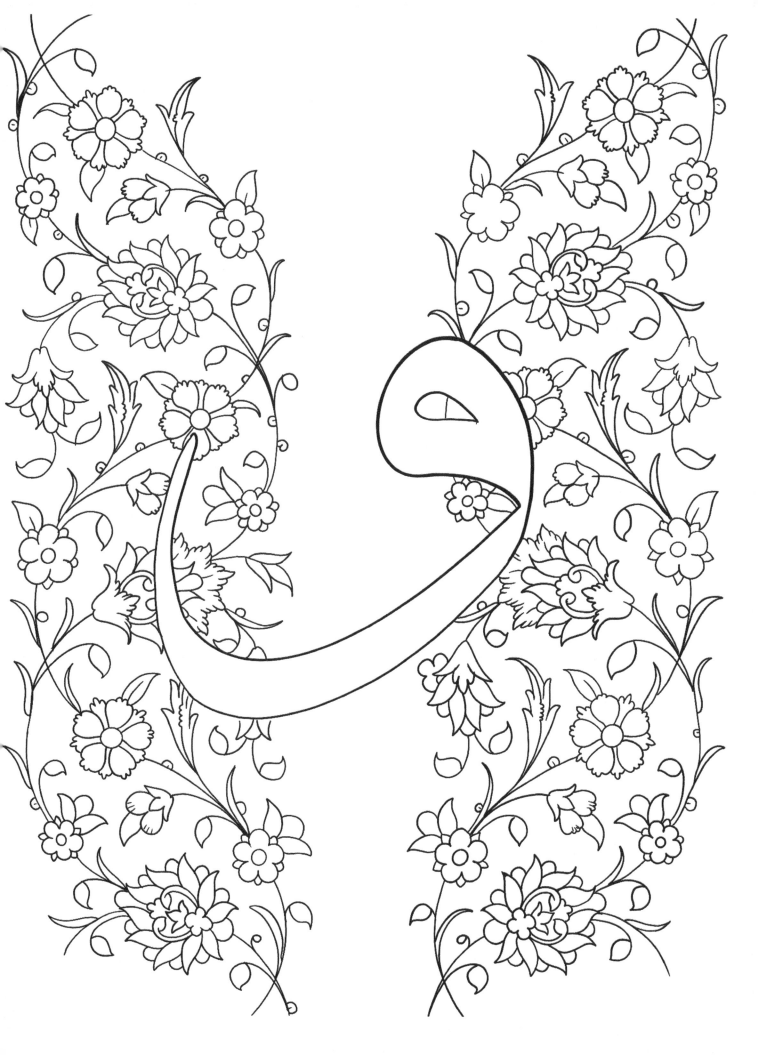

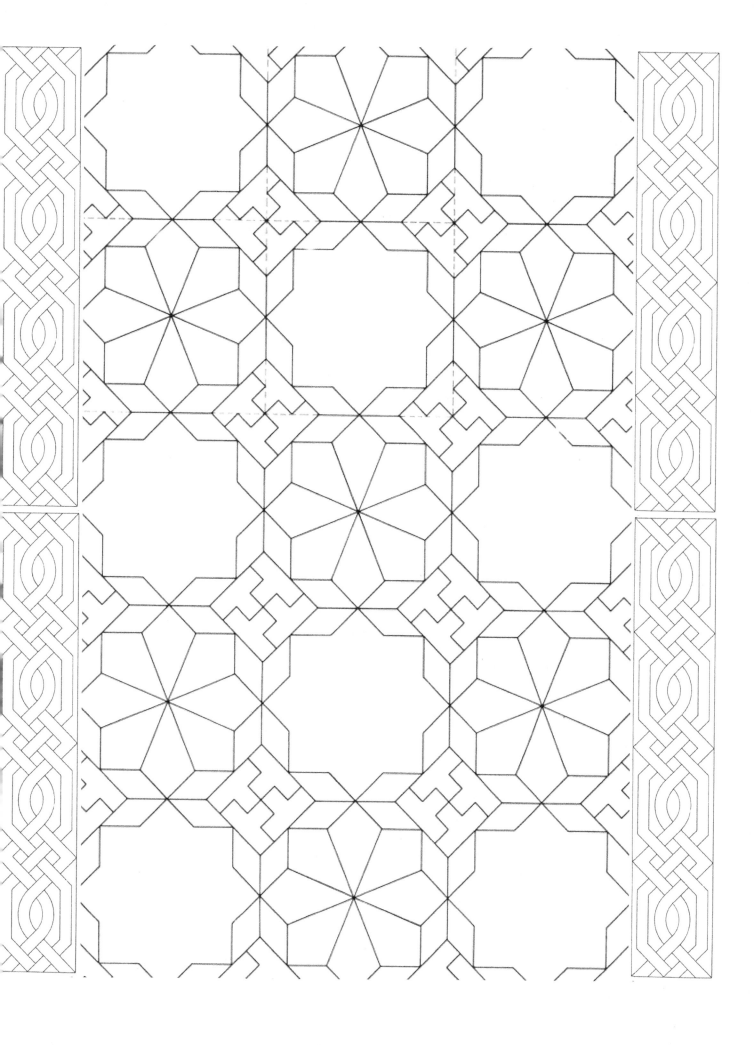

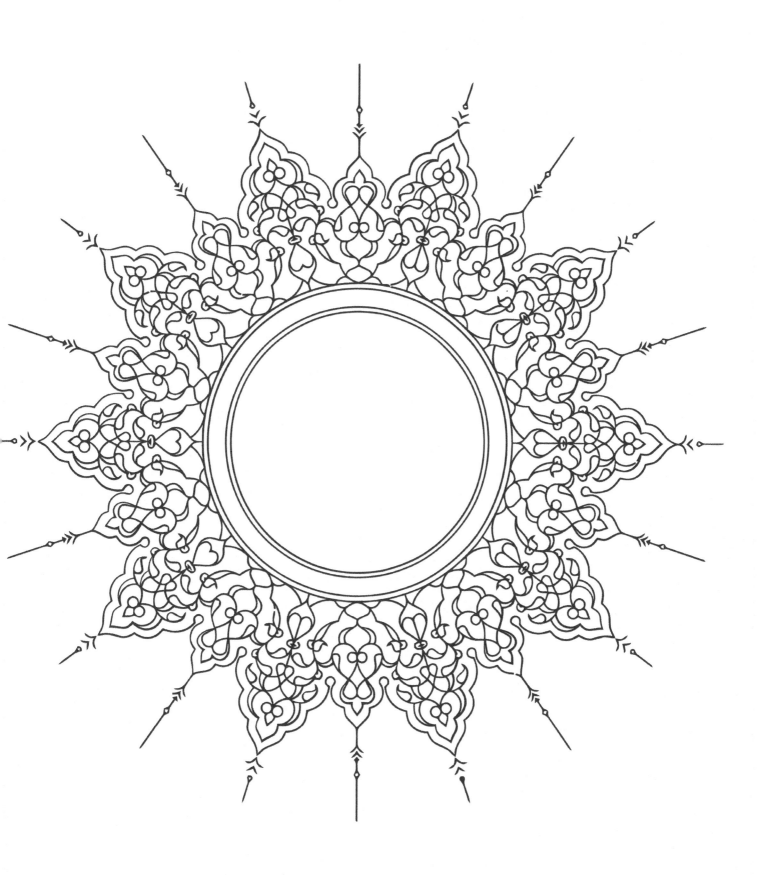

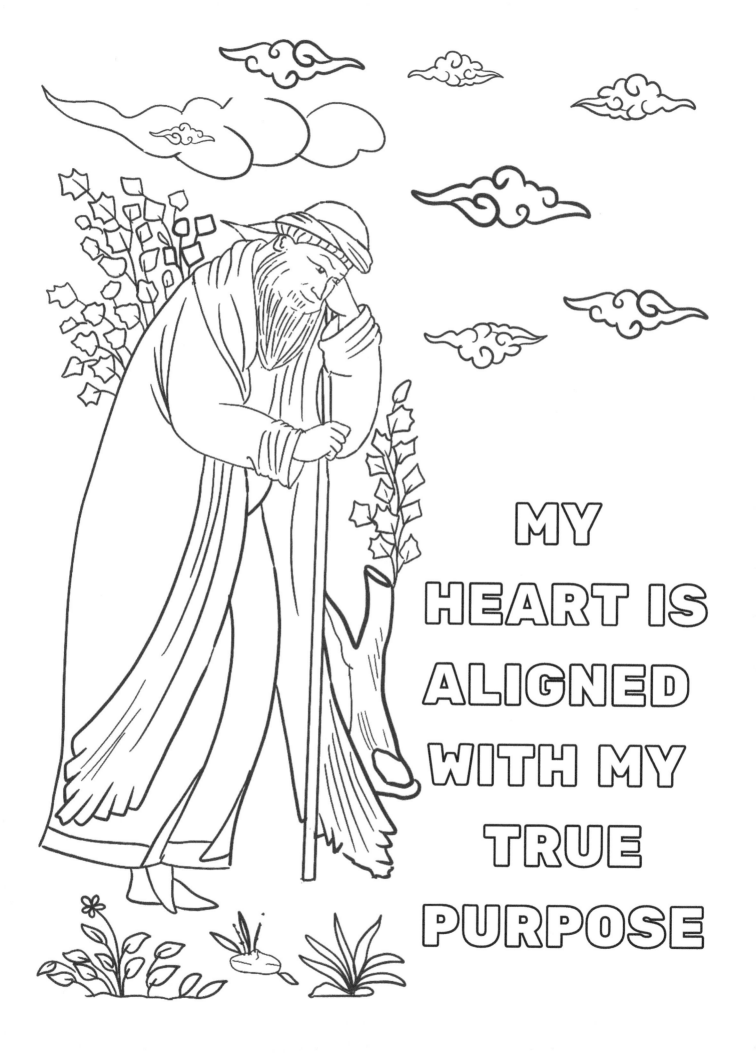

MY HEART IS ALIGNED WITH MY TRUE PURPOSE

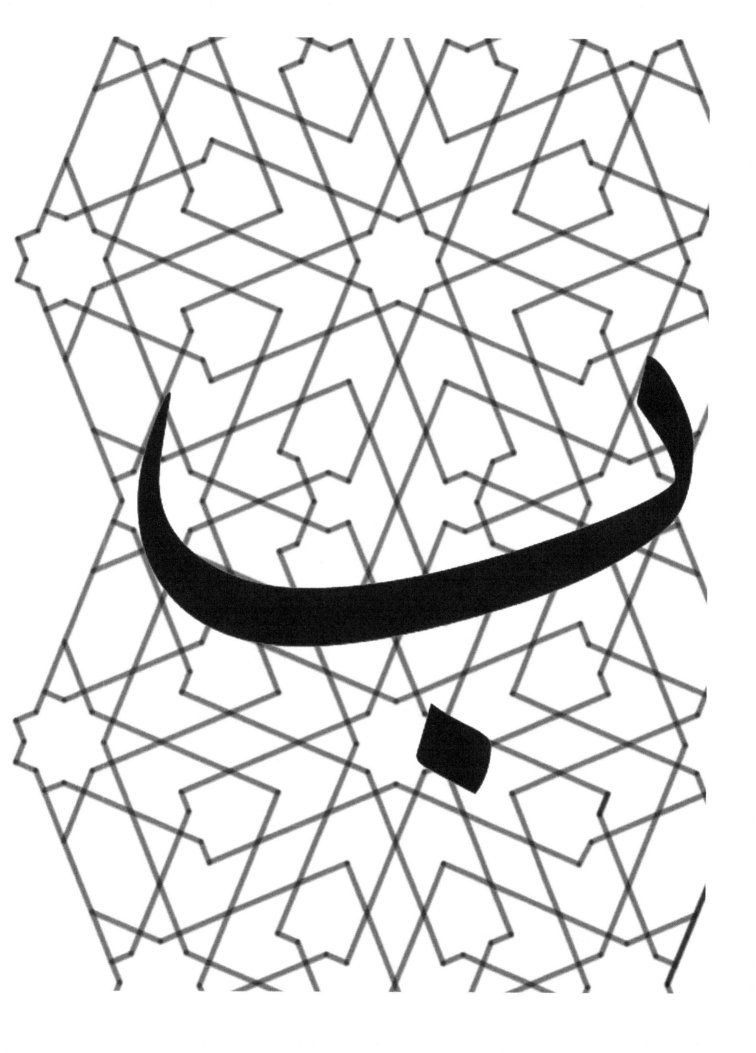

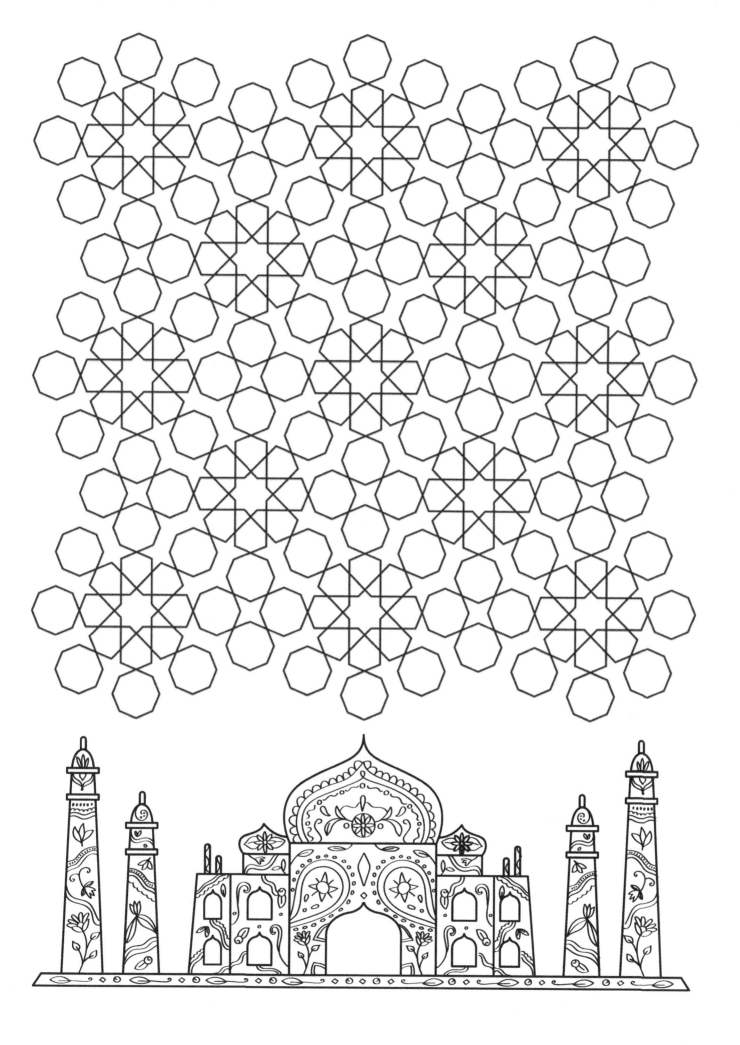

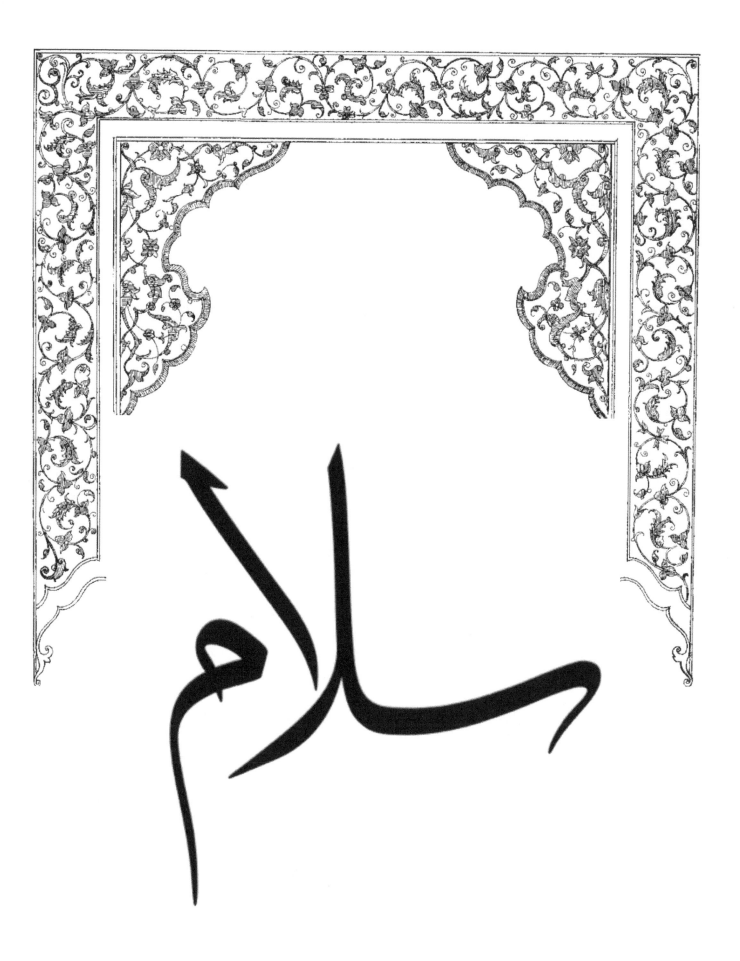

سلام

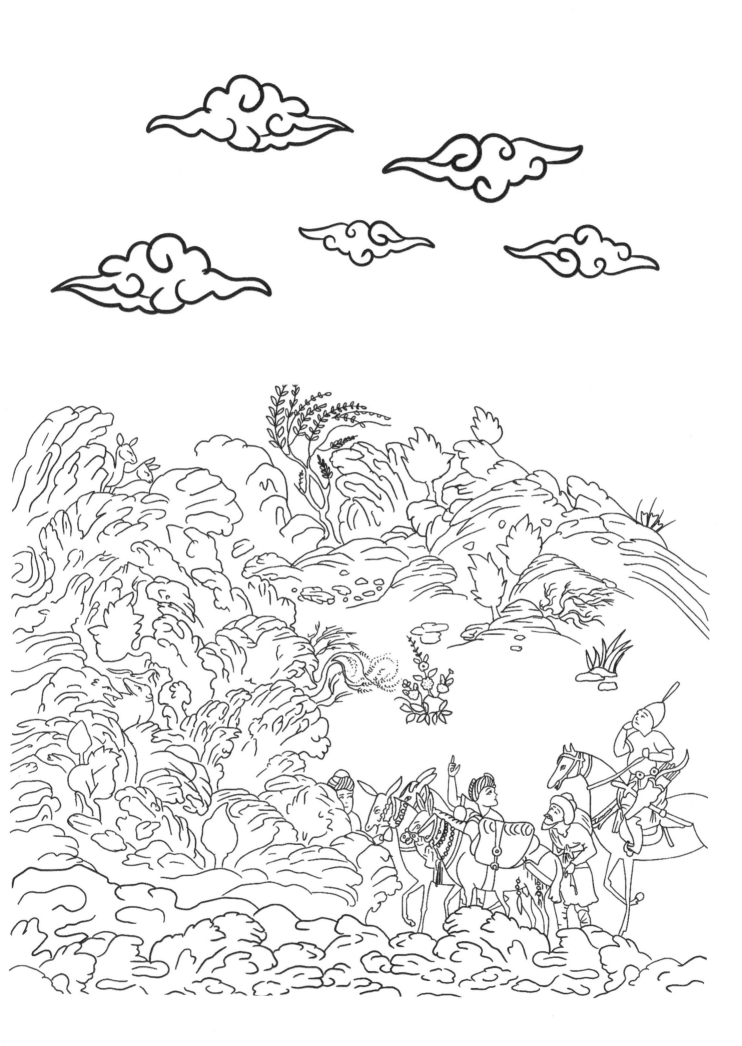

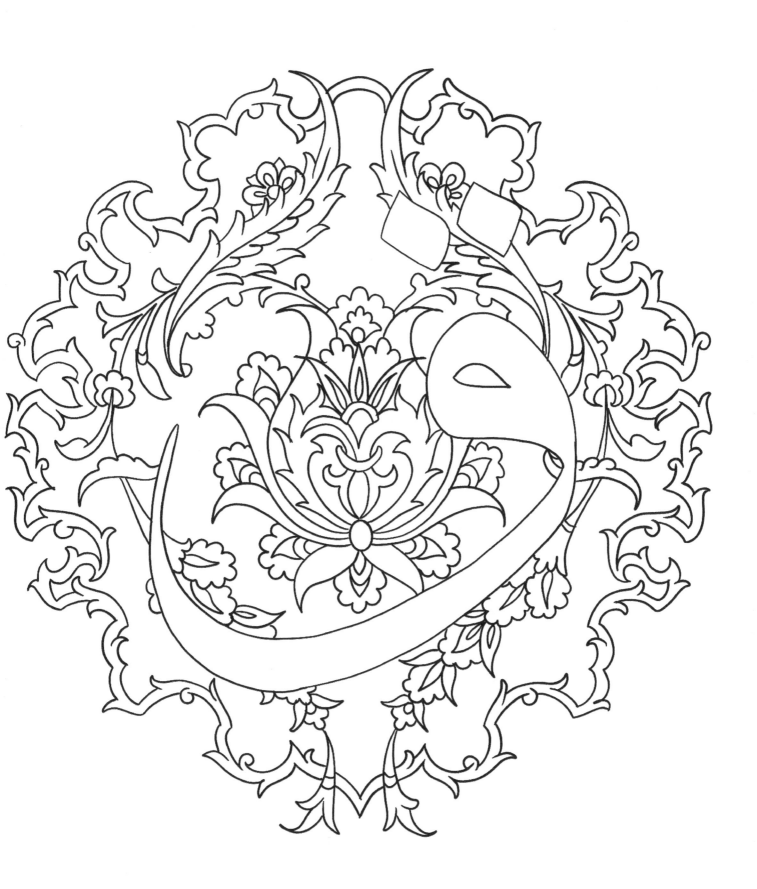

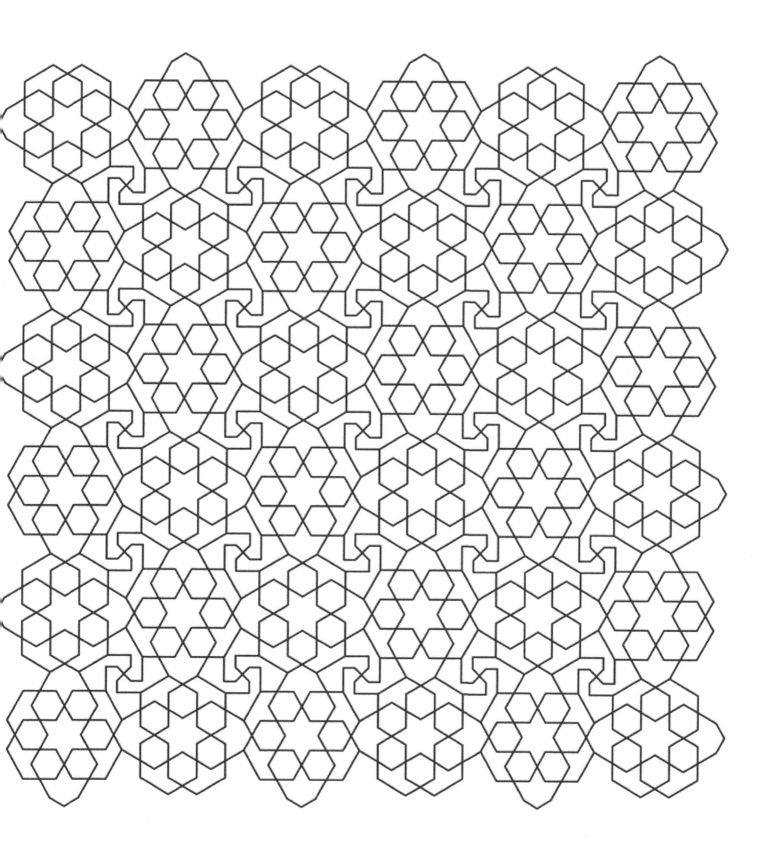

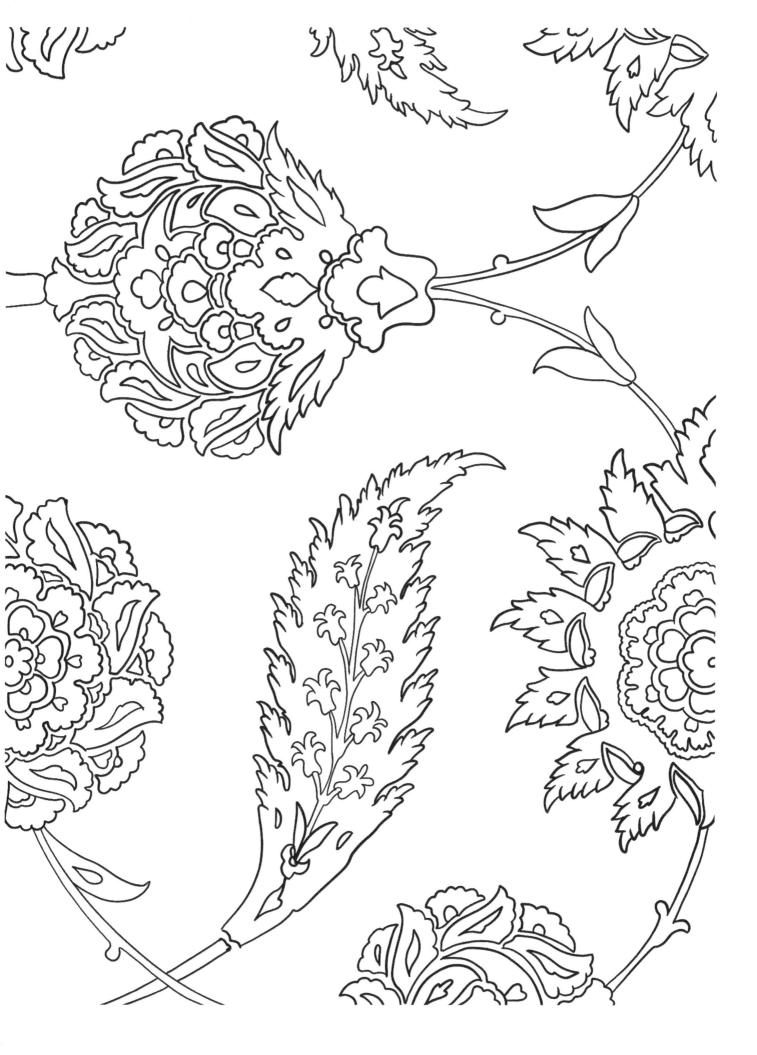

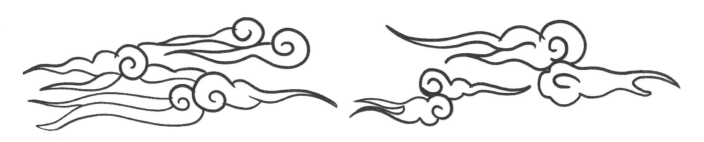

MY HEART WILL LEAD ME TO THE MYSTICS WAY

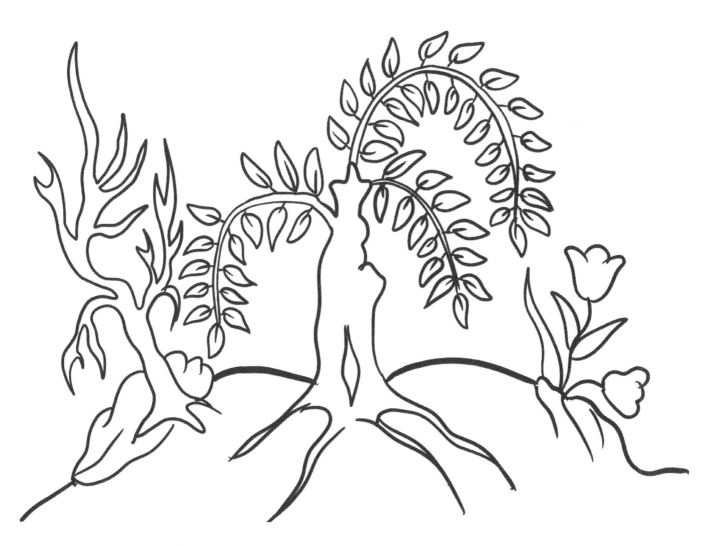

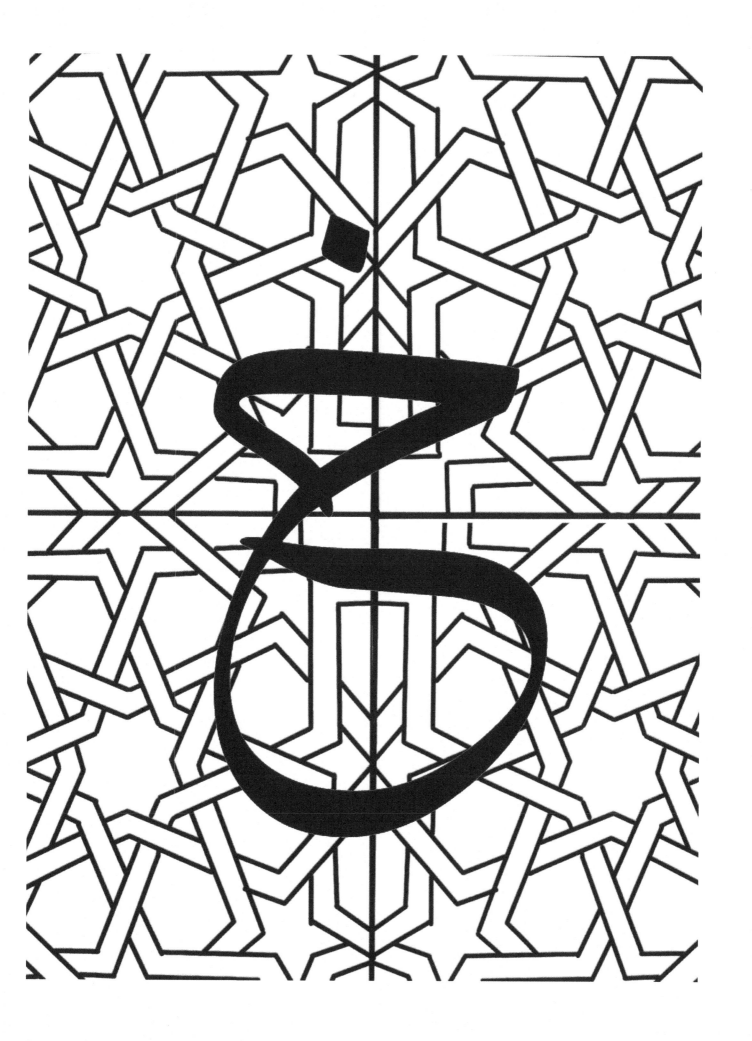

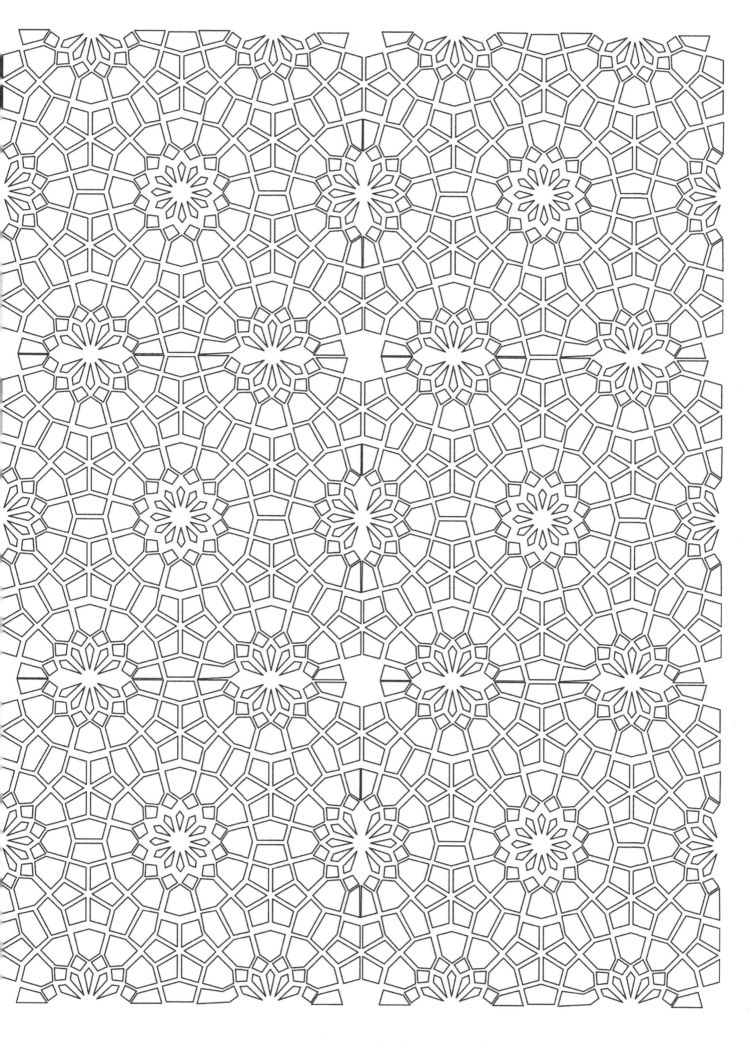

I PRACTICE LISTENING AND RESPONDING TO MY HEART'S VOICE

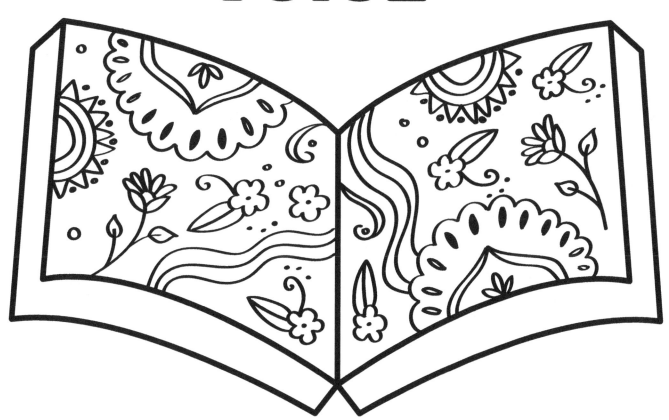

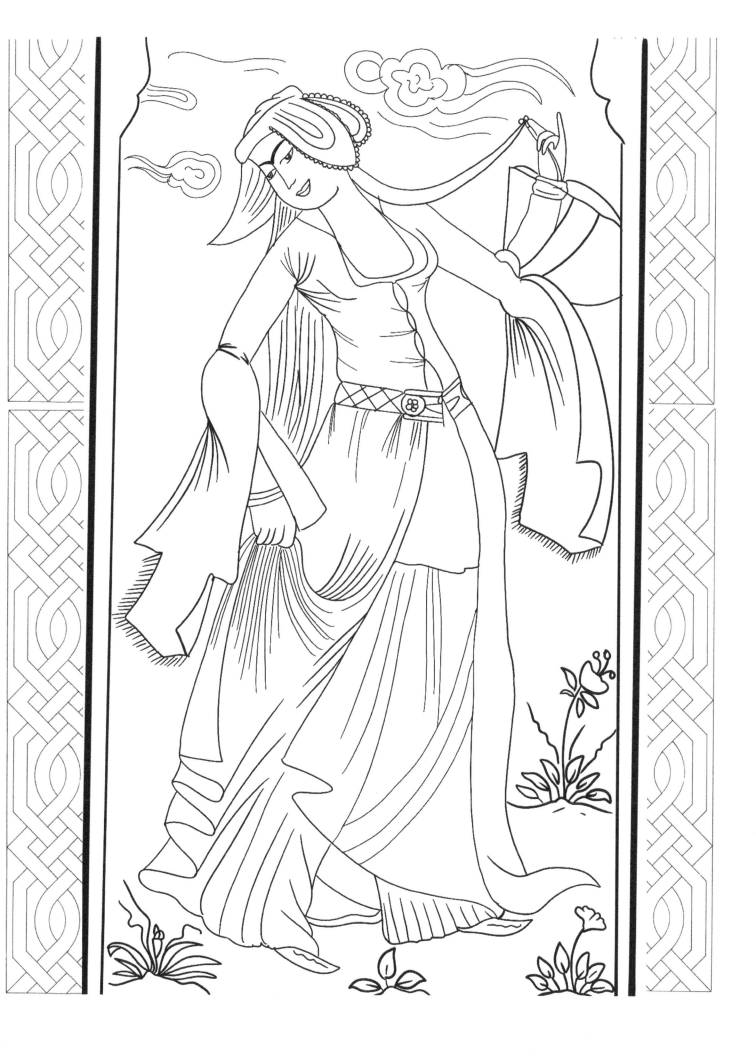

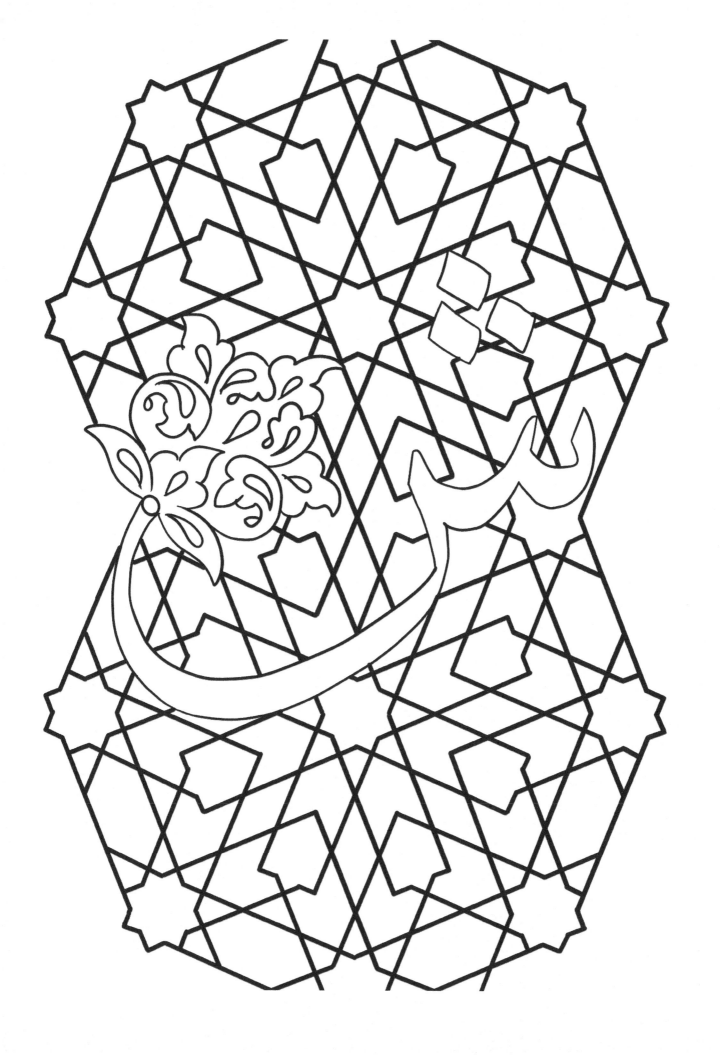

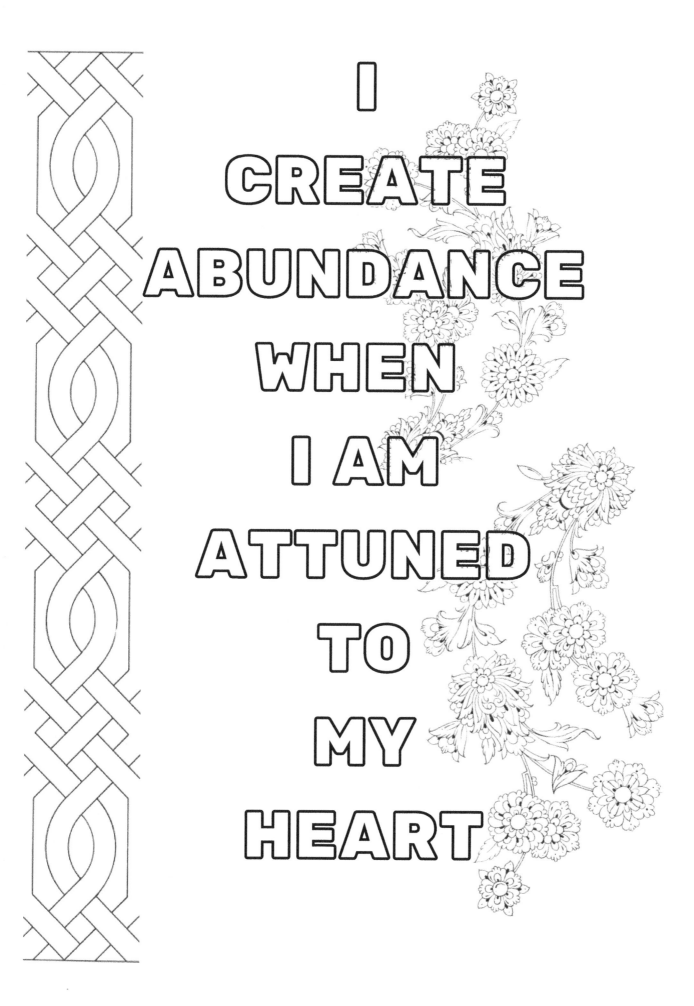

I
CREATE
ABUNDANCE
WHEN
I AM
ATTUNED
TO
MY
HEART

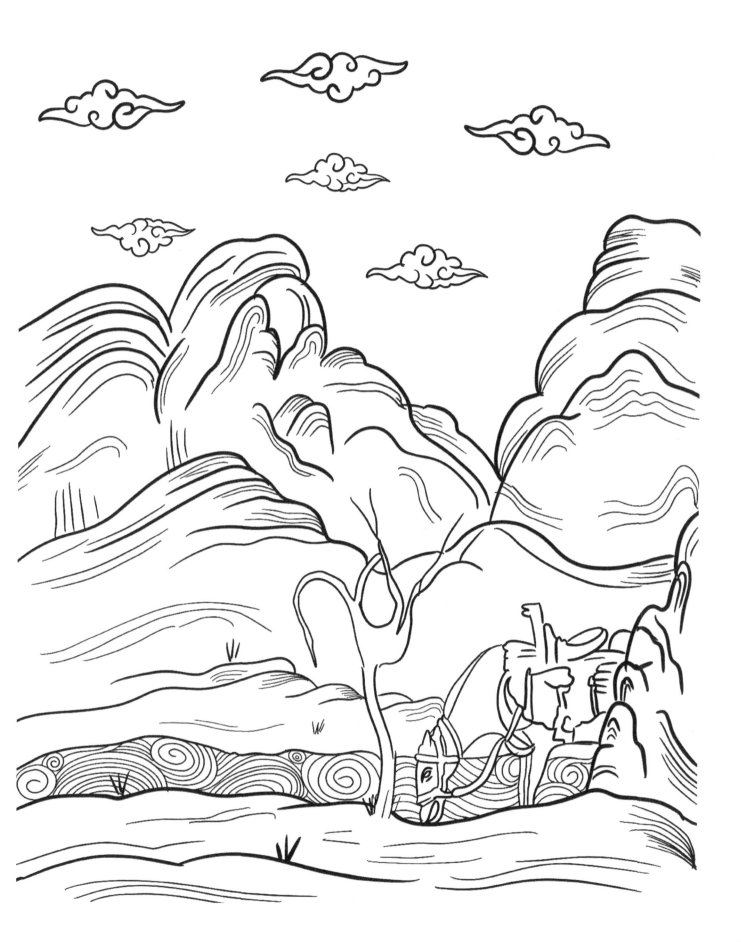

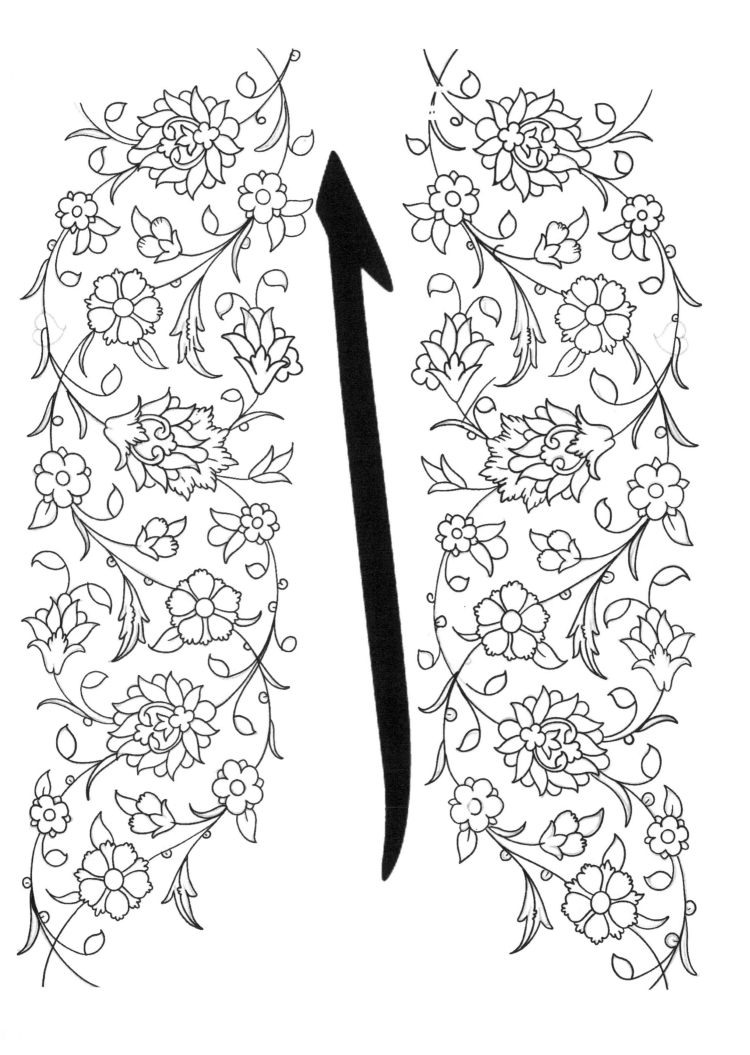

WHEN I HARMONIZE TO THE RHYTHM OF MY HEART I AM MOTIVATED BY LOVE IN ALL I DO

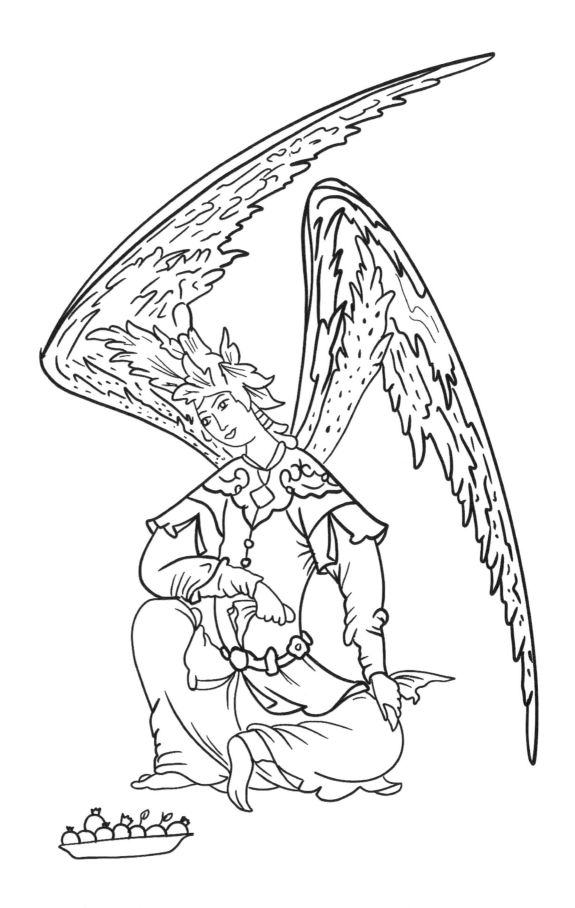

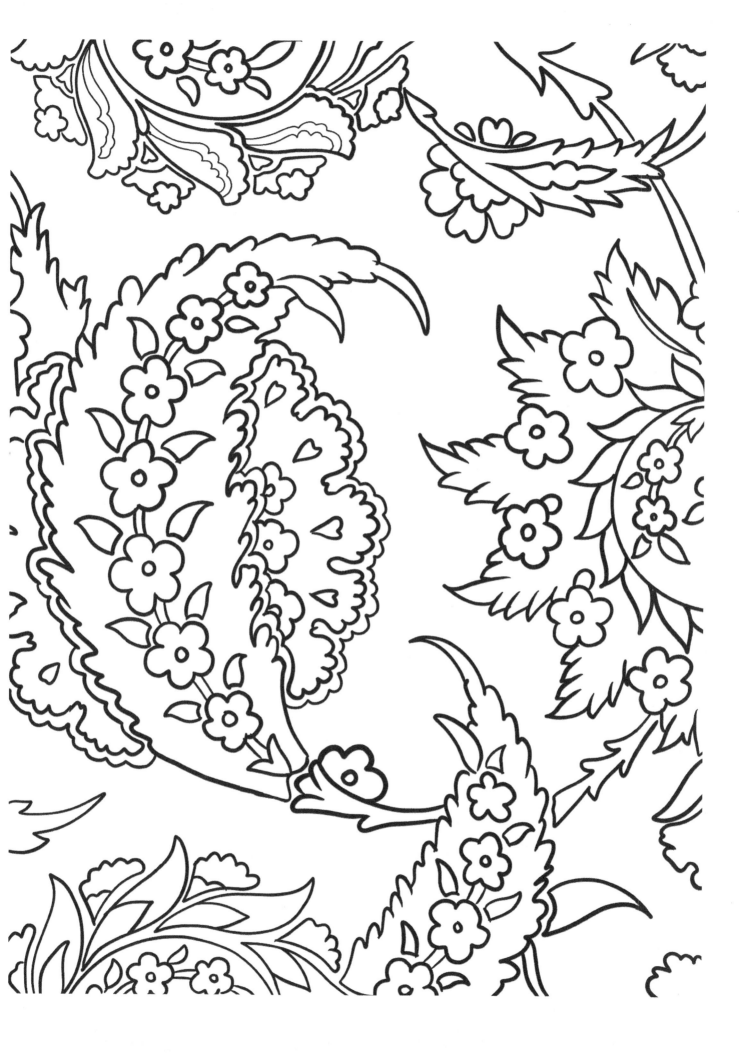

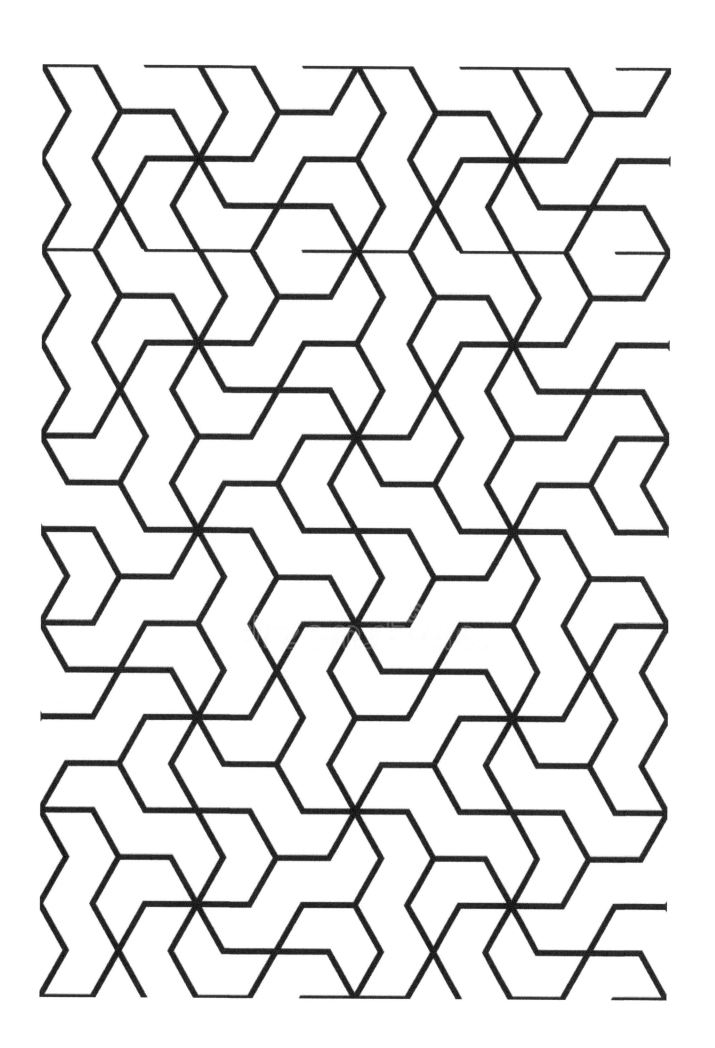

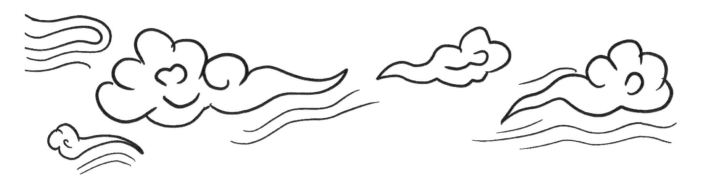
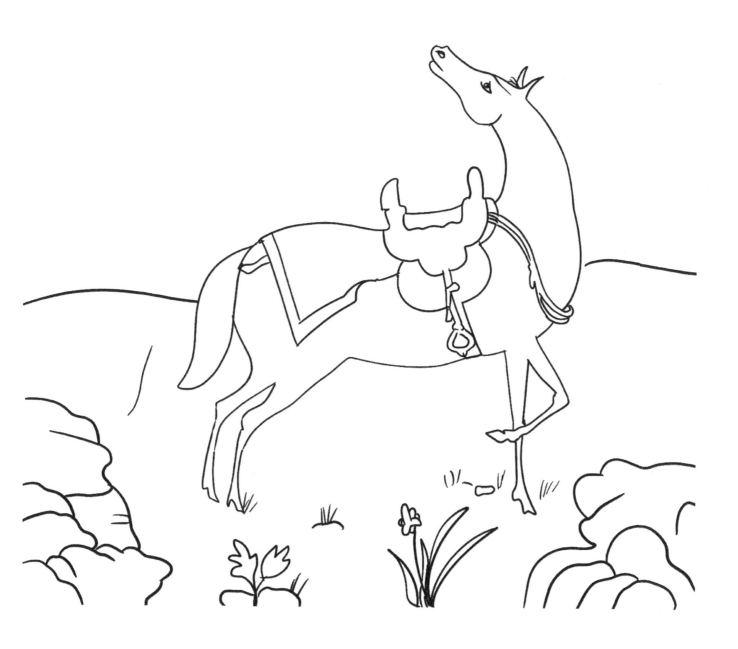

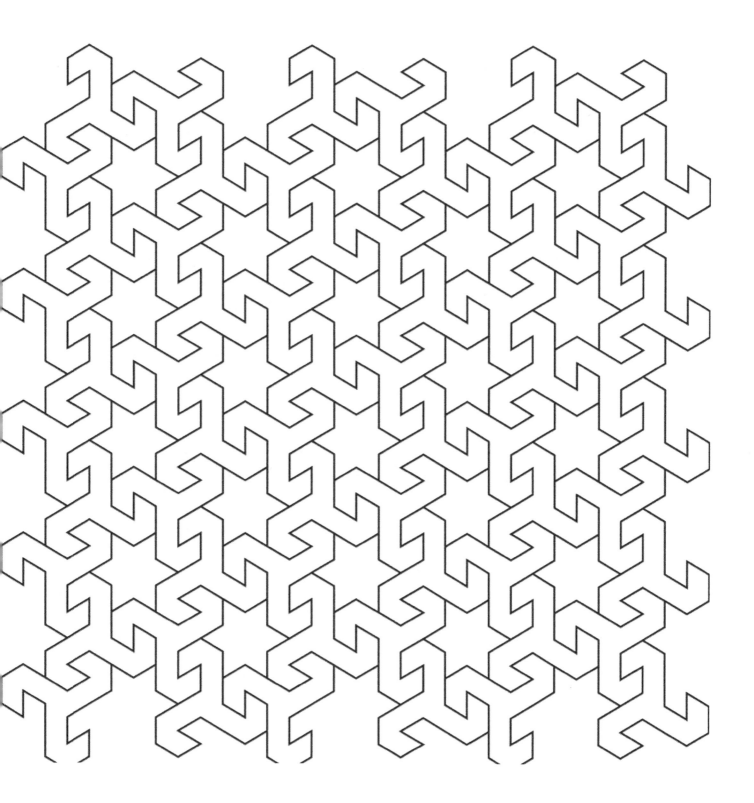

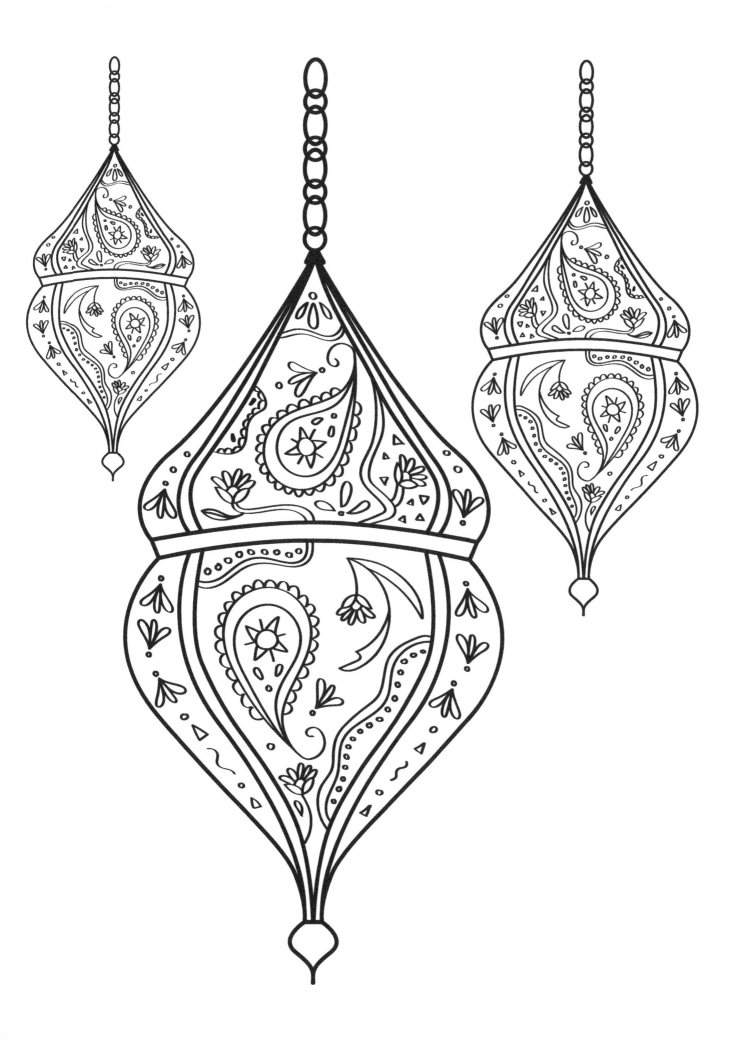

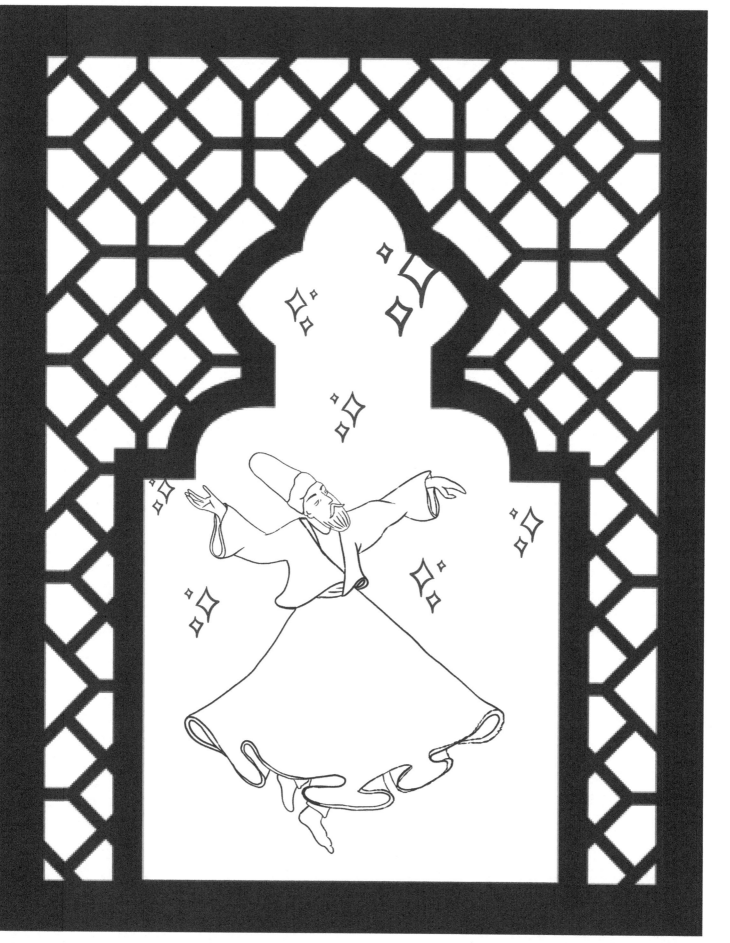

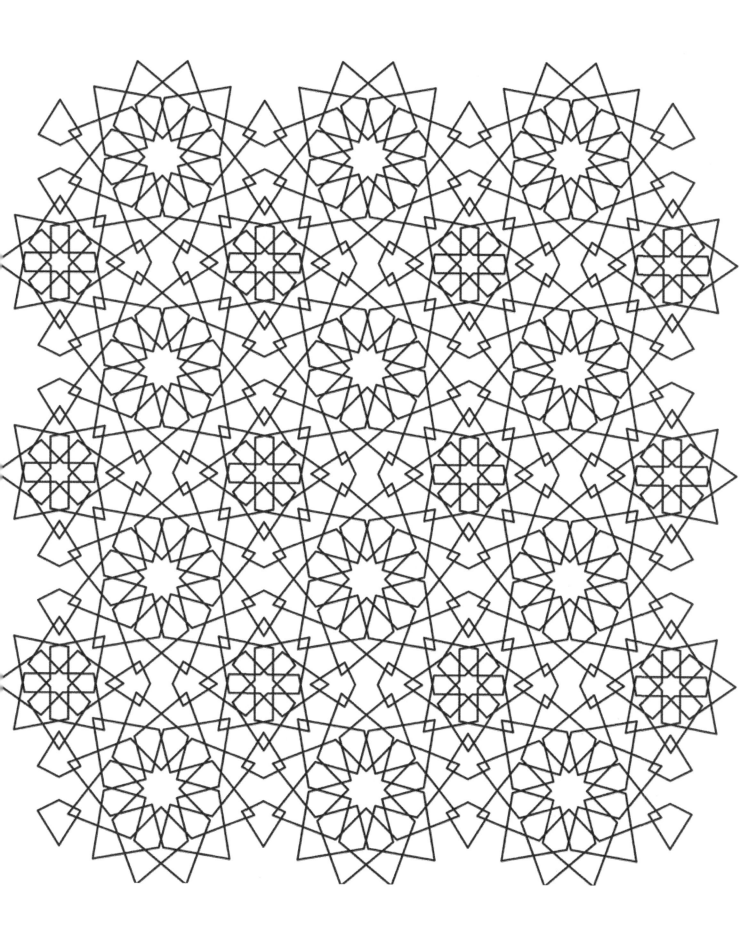

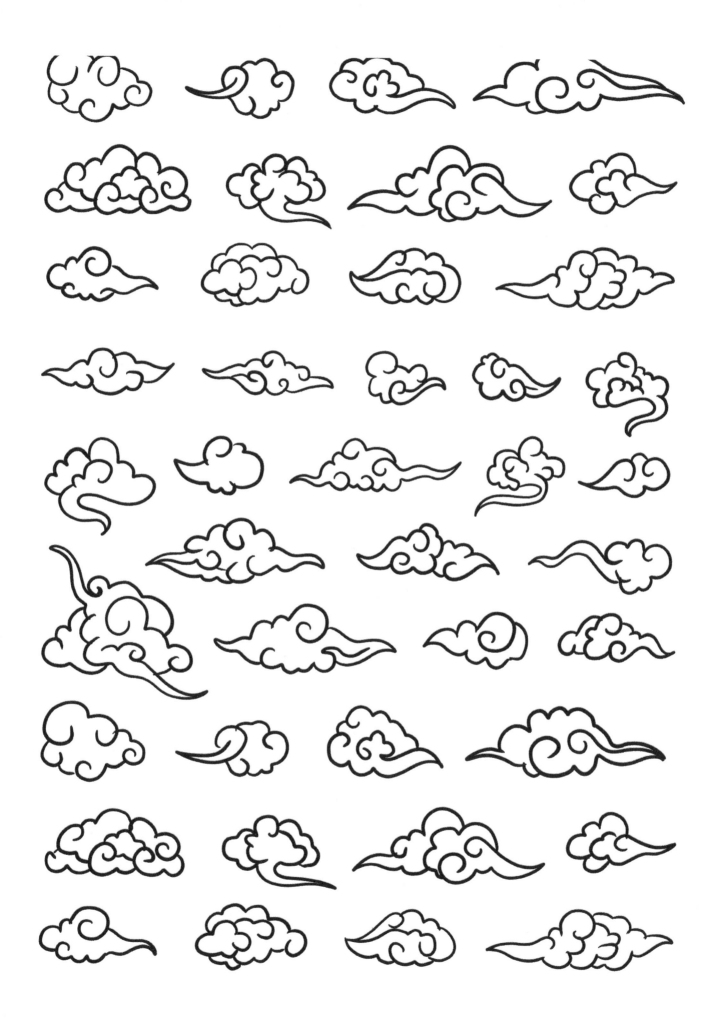

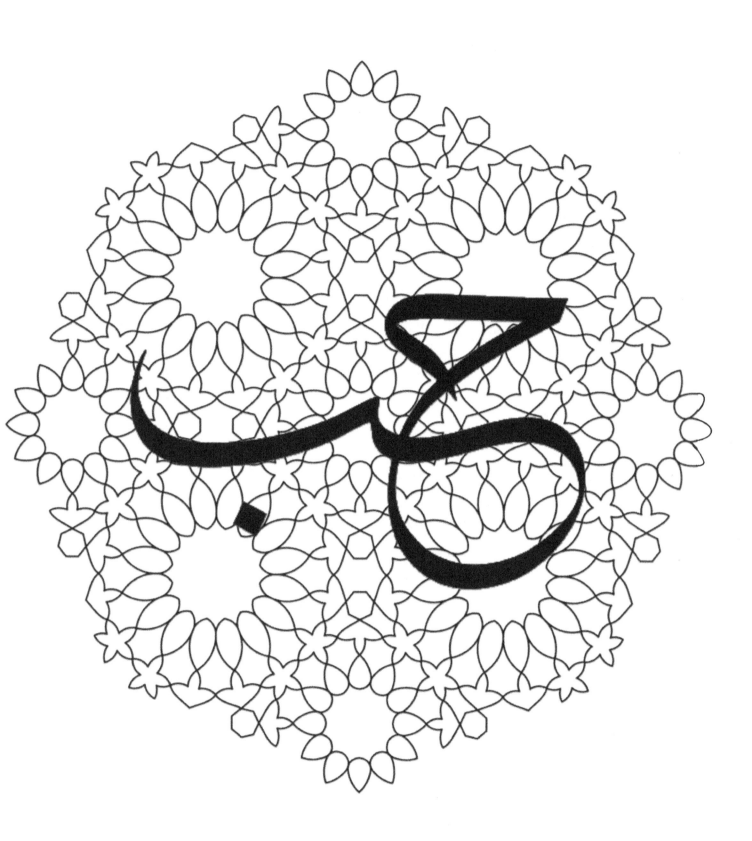

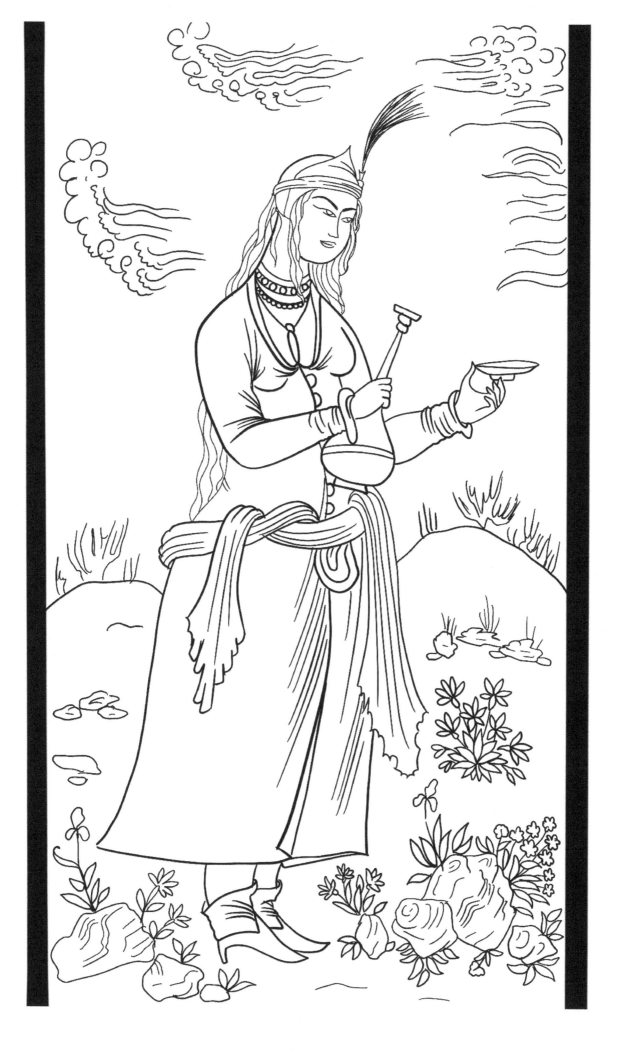

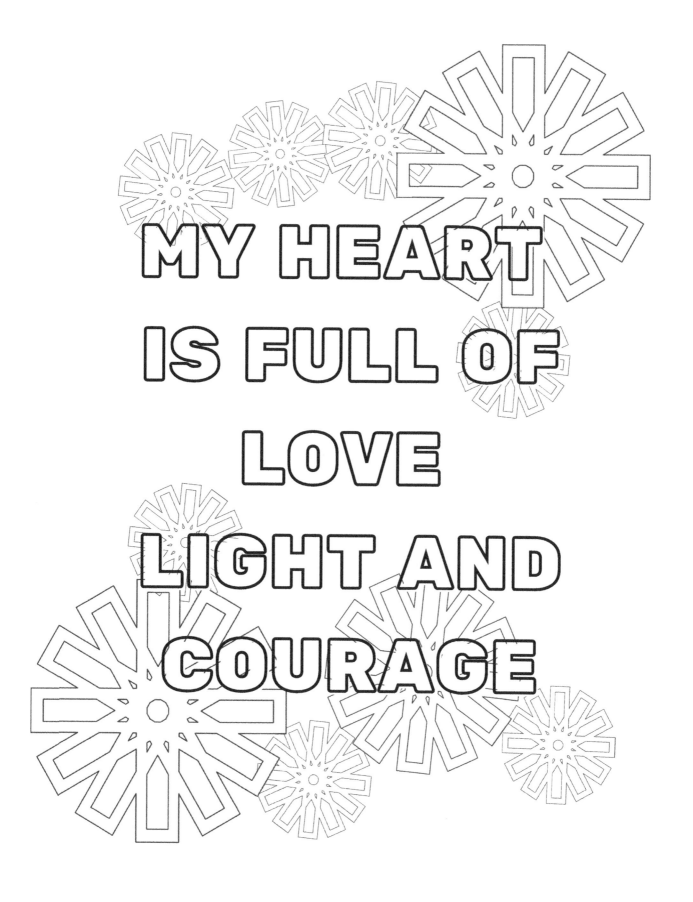

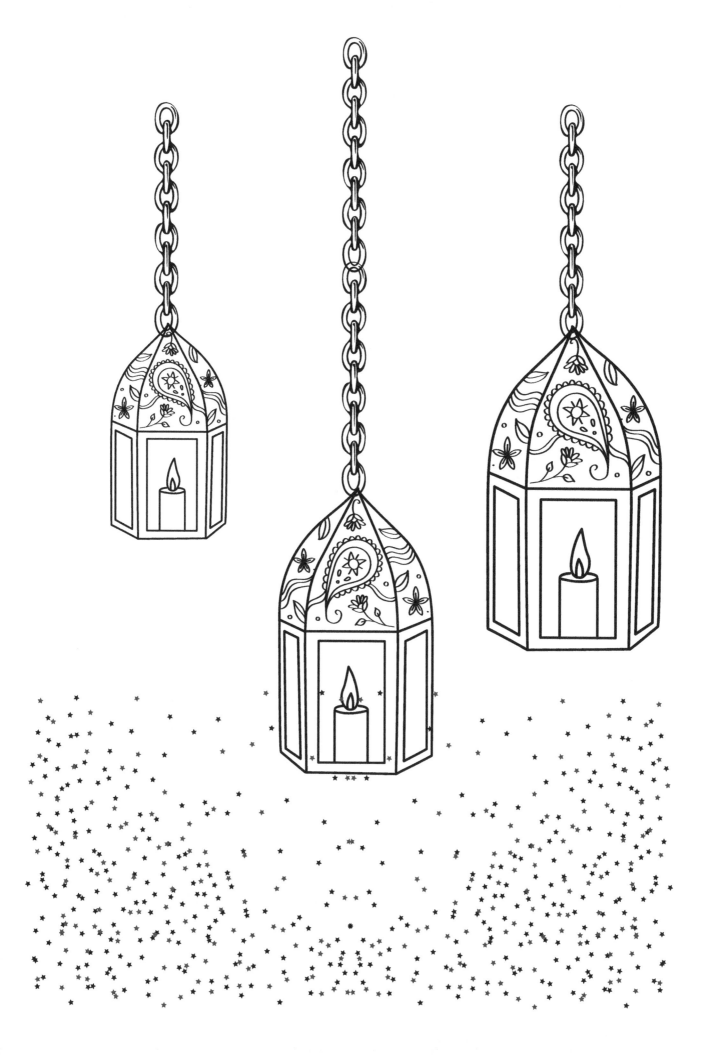

I THANK MY HEART THAT BEATS A MILLION TIMES A DAY

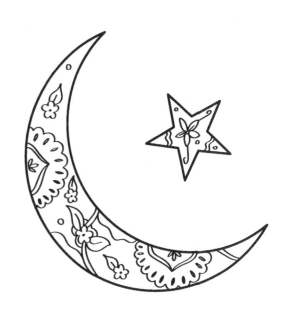

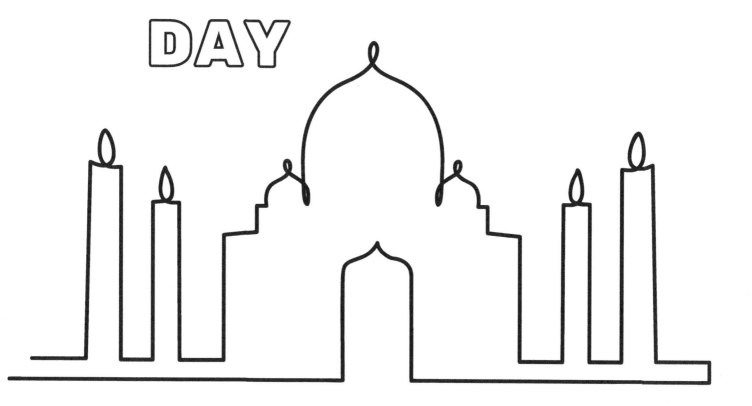

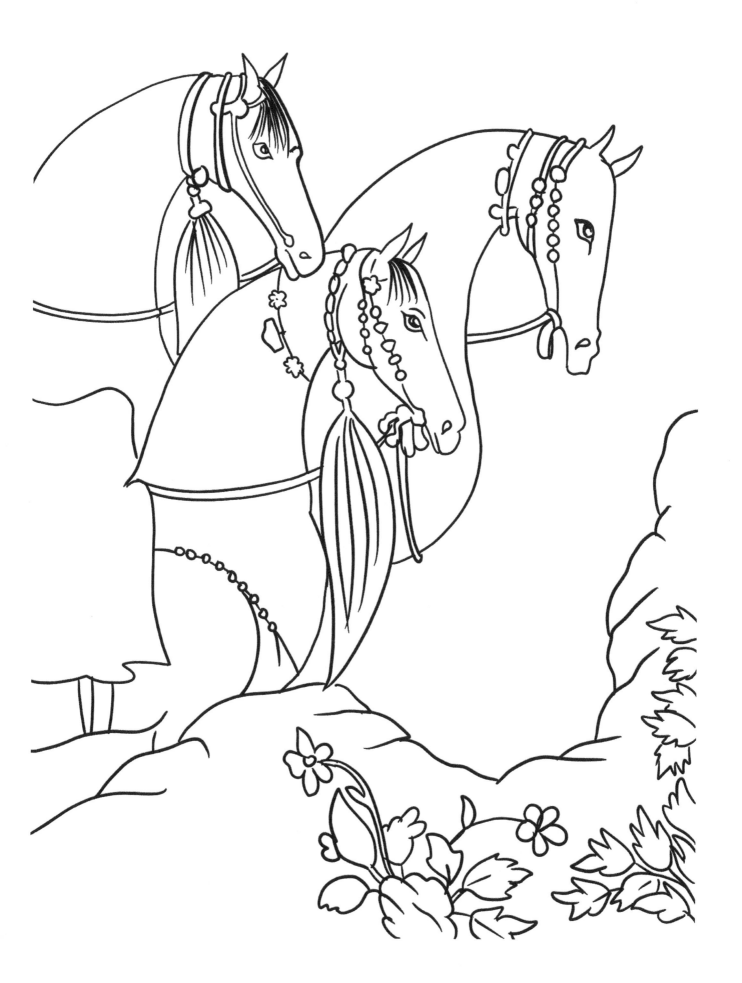

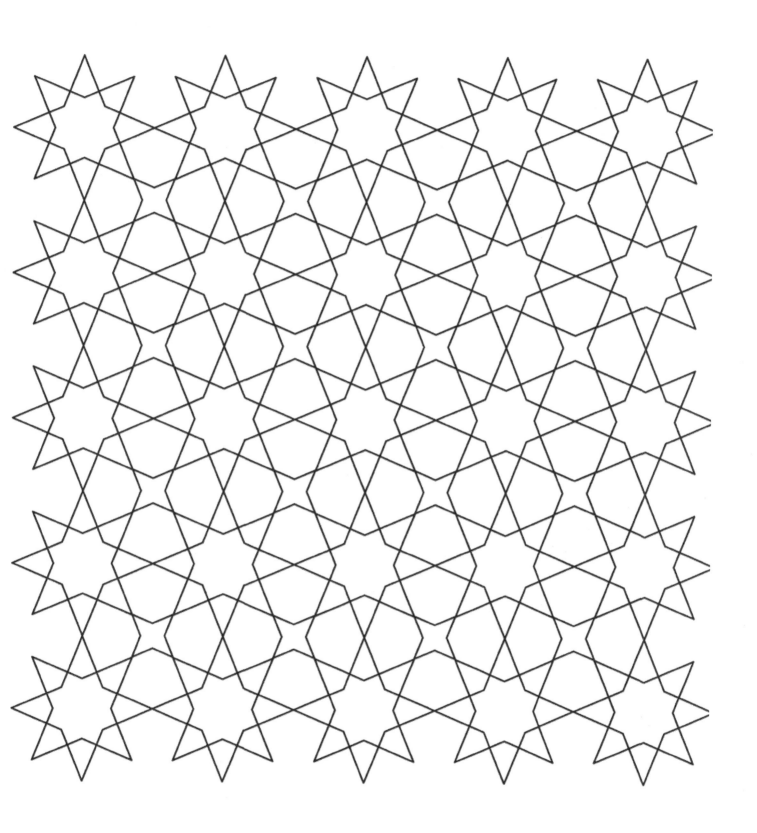

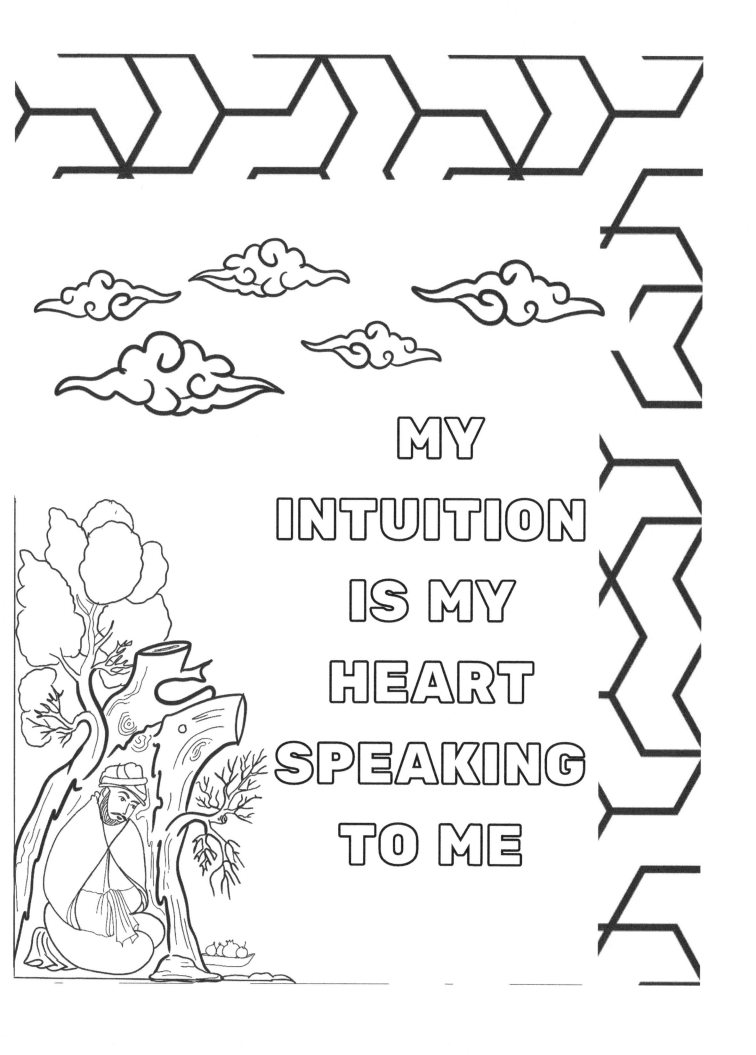

MY INTUITION IS MY HEART SPEAKING TO ME

THE
SOUL'S
FOOD
IS
WHAT
MAKES
THE
HEART
ENDURE
SO
I FEED
IT ALL
THAT IS
PURE

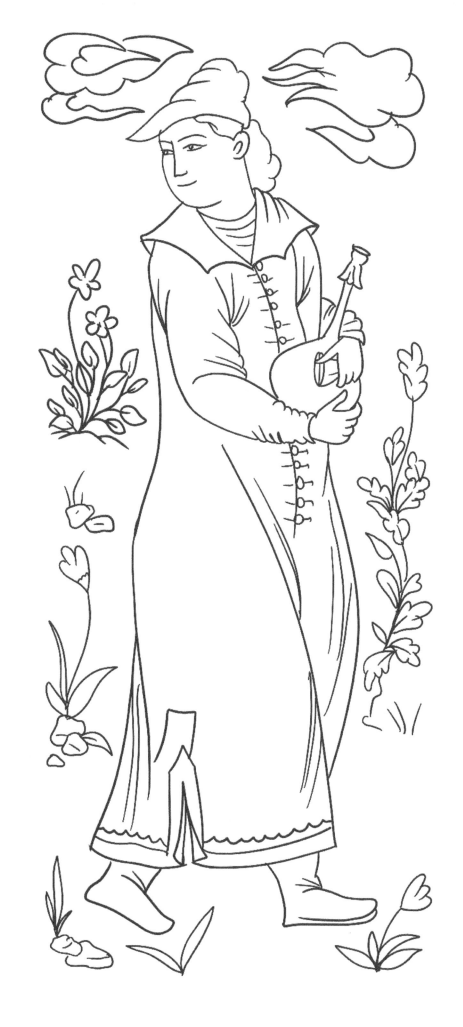

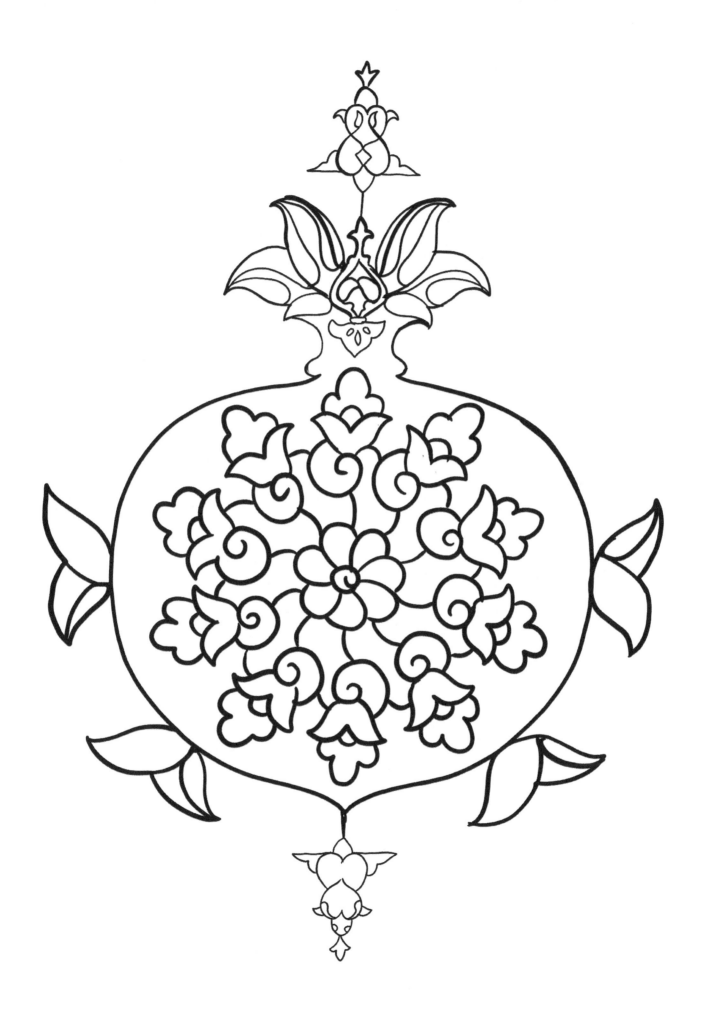

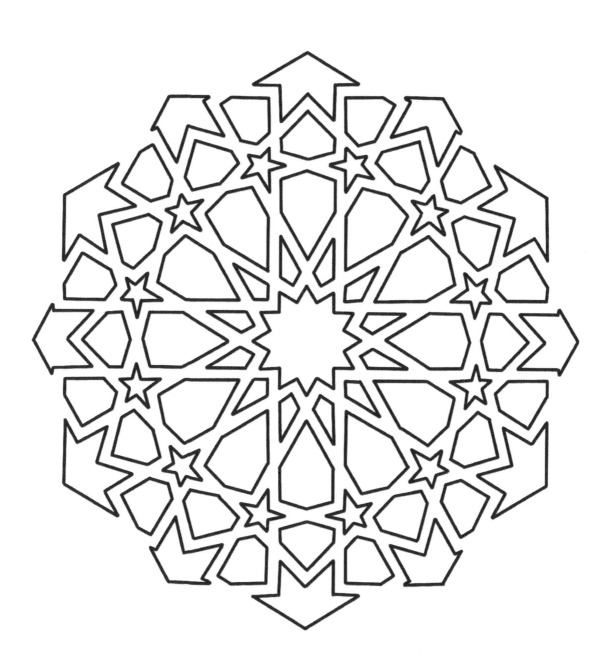

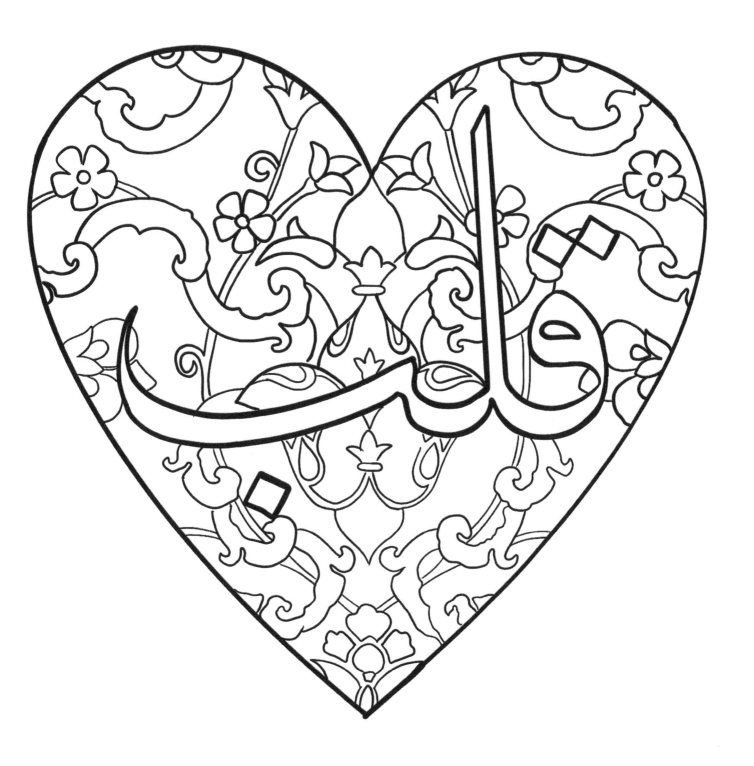